AWESOME ANNUAL

This book belongs to:

Contents

Who Died and Made You King?

Being a ruler looks like a great job – but how do you actually get to be one?
The usual answer is "My dad died and made me king."
But as you are about to find out, this can lead to all sorts of problems…

Incredible Al

Meet the mighty-but-mean Alexander the Great – he created
an empire, then died in a state!

Teachers might say Alexander was the greatest Greek ever. But they'd be doubly wrong. Alex wasn't Greek – he was a Macedonian. And the greatest? Well, in a way.

Around 330 BC, Al led his army on an awesome military campaign through western Asia and turned this huge area into his very own empire – all before he reached the age of 32!

If you believe some of the stories people told about him, Alex was a god in human form who went everywhere with his best pal and his favourite horse, murdered his mates, married a beautiful princess, wore ladies' dresses in battle … and died after a ten-day party! The truth is, incredible Al was also incredibly awful.

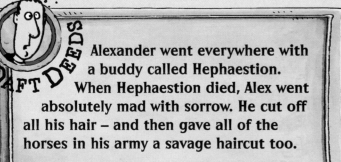

DAFT DEEDS

Alexander went everywhere with a buddy called Hephaestion. When Hephaestion died, Alex went absolutely mad with sorrow. He cut off all his hair – and then gave all of the horses in his army a savage haircut too.

WHEN ALEX ATTACKS

HORRIBLE HAPPENINGS

If more people knew about Alexander the Great's gruesome deeds, maybe they wouldn't think he was so great after all…

TYRE TORTURER
It took Alex eight tough months to take the city of Tyre in the eastern Mediterranean. Afterwards he relaxed … by having 2,000 Tyrians crucified on the city's beaches.

PERSIAN PUNISHER
After capturing Gaza (south of Tyre), Al grabbed the city's governor. He had the man tied to a horse and then dragged through the streets.

THAT'S HIM BROUGHT TO HEEL

WHAT A DRAG!

MATE MANGLER
Alex got drunk one evening … and killed his friend Cleitus with a spear. Why? Because Cleitus said kind things about Alex's dad – and Alex got jealous!

BOY BEATER
Once, after a boar hunt, Alex had a boy whipped – for killing a boar before Alex managed to! (The boy had only killed it because it was charging at Alex.) The boy was so upset, he and some others plotted to kill Alex – but Alex found out and had them killed. What a boar!

...and a Fierce Foe

DARIUS III

Alex's main enemy was Darius, king of Persia. (The Persians were the top power in the ancient world – that is, until Alexander came along.)

Tall tyrant

Darius was a huge man – he stood head-and-shoulders above his men in battle. So it's not surprising that his throne was king-sized, too. When Alex sat on it (after he'd conquered Persia) his feet didn't reach the ground.

Women at war

Persian royal women were very important, so Darius took his mum, sister, wife and daughters everywhere – even into battle! (He also took 360 girlfriends – one for each day of the Persian year.) When Darius lost a battle with Alexander at Issus in Syria, he escaped – but Alex captured his ladies. Hundreds of Persian women must have been a handful!

Darius should have known the Battle of Issus would be a washout. He had asked one adviser, named Charidemus, to speak his mind honestly about who was more likely to win. Unhappily for Chari, Darius didn't like bad news...

Scarpering king

Darius and Alexander's final showdown was at the Battle of Gaugamela. Darius assembled a vast army ... but ran away and hid when things started to go wrong! A band of his own men found him but turned traitor and murdered him!

NOSEY NO LONGER

The traitors' leader, Bessus, crowned himself king ... but not for long. Alex caught up with him and gave him the Persian punishment reserved for king-killers. He had Bessus' ears and nose sliced off.

9

Rome Sweet Rome

The Evil Emperors

You may have thought Julius Caesar was a bit full of himself, but some of the other emperors were a hundred times worse. Here are a few of the rottenest Romans who ever lived...

Tiberius AD 14–37

Favourite saying: "I don't care if they hate me so long as they obey me!" (Sound like any teachers you may know?) Unfortunately, Tiberius, unlike your teacher, had the nasty habit of breaking the legs of anyone who disobeyed him.

Rottenest act: He had a poor fisherman stripped and skinned alive – using a scaly fish and the sharp shell of a crab. His crime? Bringing the emperor a present when he didn't want to be disturbed.

Sticky end: Suffocated – probably by one of his helpers.

DID YOU KNOW...?

Rome's emperors were a funny bunch. Here are some of their lesser-known nasty habits and potty hobbies...

• Emperor Vitellius AD 69 (known as 'The Glutton') only ruled for a matter of months before he was dragged half-naked to the Forum where he was tortured, killed and tossed in the River Tiber. Even so, by Evil Emperor standards, he wasn't that cruel (although he did starve his mother to death!)

Vitellius stuffed himself three times a day. At one of his banquets, 2,000 fish and 7,000 birds were served. He liked to snack on pike livers, pheasant brains and flamingo tongues.

• Emperor Domitian's (AD 81–96) hobby was inventing new ways of torture – his favourite was barbecuing people's naughty bits. In his spare time, he liked catching flies and tearing off their wings.

• In contrast, Emperor Heliogabalus' favourite hobby was positively kind to flies. He liked collecting cobwebs ... by the ton!

OF ALL MY BELGIAN COBWEBS THIS IS MY FAVOURITE

Caligula   AD 37–41

Favourite saying: "Rome is a city of necks just waiting for me to chop."

Rottenest acts: Caligula enjoyed nothing more than a good blood bath in the arena. But the wild animals had to be kept alive until the day of the show. This was very expensive, so Caligula found a cheap supply of raw meat for them ... he fed the animals on criminals!

He can't have been all bad, as he loved his sister Drusilla very much (rumour has it he married her!). When she died, he made the whole empire mourn for a year. Anyone who laughed, ate with his own family or took a bath was executed.

Sticky end: For the first six months of his reign, Caligula was so popular that when he fell ill all of Rome went into mourning. But they got even sadder when he recovered!

Nice Caligula had gone stark raving bonkers. In the end one of his guards stabbed him to death.

Caligula is supposed to have threatened to make his dear friend Incitatus a consul. This would make Incitatus one of the most powerful rulers in the Roman Empire. So what? Well, Incitatus was his favourite horse!

DID YOU KNOW...?

• Emperor Caligula's real name was Gaius. Caligula was just a nickname meaning 'little boot'. This was because, as a child, he liked dressing up and playing at being a soldier from a very early age.

• Caligula wanted to copy Julius Caesar and invade Britain.

In AD 40 he went to the Roman base in northern France where he set sail to lead the invasion. He turned back when he saw that no-one wanted to follow him!

Not wanting to return home empty handed, he ordered his soldiers to gather seashells from the beach and sent them to Rome as spoils of war!

Claudius   AD 41–54

Favourite saying: "K-k-k-k-k-...er...execute him!"

Rottenest acts: When Claudius discovered that his wife was a bit of a flirt and had wild parties with her friends, he was not too happy. He had his fun-loving missus executed but he also got rid of 300 of her pesky party friends!

Sticky end: Cruel Claudius was poisoned with mushrooms.

DID YOU KNOW…?

Because he had a stammer, Claudius' family thought he was an idiot. (He wasn't.) His nephew, Caligula, made fun of him in public. So, Claudius' promotion came as a bit of a surprise … especially to him! The guards who murdered Caligula found Claudius hiding behind a curtain – then declared him emperor!

Nero   AD 54–68

Favourite saying: He played the lyre very badly but people told him he was good. When he knew he had to die all he could say was "What a loss I shall be to the art of music!"

Rottenest acts: Murdering people, including his own mother! He had his half-brother, Britannicus, poisoned. Britannicus had a food taster who ate and drank a bit of every dish. If it was poisoned, the taster's sensitive taste buds would taste the poison. The taster drank some hot wine – it was safe. Britannicus took it and added some water to cool it. Then he drank it … and died. The water had been poisoned!

Sticky end: When he knew the army had deserted him and rebels were coming to get him, he placed a sword to his throat. One of his friends gave him a push. He bled to death.

Foul Facts

Christians brought out Nero's nastiest side. He had them covered in animal skins and thrown to hungry dogs. Or sometimes he would make his own special Roman candles: take one Christian, tie him to a post, cover in tar and set alight.

PHEW!

The Colosseum

The Romans liked their entertainment to be deadly. Their top venue for fierce fun was the Colosseum. On a show day, its arena would be filled with roars, paws and gore...

In AD106 Emperor Trajan held games lasting 117 days. Over 9,000 gladiators were killed.

The emperor often gave out lottery tickets to the crowd. You might end up rich, but were more likely to win a booby prize – like a dead dog.

Criminals fought beasts in the morning, executions were held during lunch, while the 'pro' gladiators hacked each other up in the afternoon.

To make sure no-one faked death in the arena, a man dressed as Dis, the god of the dead, bonked any fallen combatants over the head with a hammer. Then another helpful attendant, dressed as Mercury, went round prodding the bodies with a red hot poker!

NOW I'M STUMPED!

The Lion Keeper
A story by Terry Deary

Emperor Nero stinks of perfume. He wears a sickly sweet scent of flowers. It hides the smell of the sweat and the blood and the animals that are dying under his fine nose. Most of all it hides the smell of the fear.

The emperor smiles at the screaming mob of Romans and waves a hand. He turns to his guard and says, "They love me. I give them a feast of death and they love me!"

He looks over the sand in the arena.

Every time it is stained with blood slaves rush in and scatter fresh sand.

The sun is warm and the sport has been good that morning. A bull and a rhino had fought fiercely until the gladiators had entered the arena to finish them off. The crowd loved that.

Starved and shabby tigers had fought wearily and a sickly crocodile had refused to fight at all. Never mind. The mob knows there'll be lots more blood before the day is done.

"What next?" Nero asks.

"A criminal will be torn apart by a lion, sir."

"I once fought a lion," Nero said.

"Yes, sir, I remember," the guard says. He remembers that the lion was old and had its teeth and claws pulled out.

An iron gate creaks and scrapes as it swings open.

A dark-haired man blinks out into the sunlight. A sharp spear pushes him into the arena and the gate clangs shut behind him.

The man looks around at the grinning faces of the thousands. His tunic is filthy and torn. He pushes back his shoulders. If he has to die he will die bravely.

"Who is the man?" Nero asks.

"An animal keeper, sir," the guard says quietly. "He worked for you here in the arena. He was one of your best workers. The animals were well kept when Marcus was their keeper."

Nero sneers. "So why are we executing him?"

The guard leaned forward and said, "He became a Christian, sir."

"Hah!" Nero snorts. "The Christians started the great fire in Rome last year, you know."

"So they say, sir."

"He deserves to die." Nero turns to the slave in the arena below him. The crowd falls silent. Nero gives a single nod. The crowd gives a single gasp. "Ahhhh!"

The gate opens, a lion pads softly on to the green-blue sand. It shakes its mane and yawns.

The man stares at it.

"Why doesn't he run?" Nero whines. "It's more sport when they run and the lions have to chase them!"

"Some of the Christians face death bravely," the guard says. "They think they will soon meet their God. They welcome death, sir."

"But what about the sport? The mob want their sport. If they don't get it they make trouble in the streets! They have to have their blood."

"They'll get that, sir."

"But they have to have the excitement of the chase as well."

Suddenly the emperor leaps to his feet. The crowd sees. It falls silent. "Run, man, run!" Nero screams.

The weary, ragged man turns to him. "God bless you and forgive you, Nero," he says in a voice with just the faintest tremble.

Nero is about to answer when there is a roar from the lion. It has seen the man and heard his voice. It turns and lopes towards him.

"Hahhhh!" the crowd breathes, waiting for the kill.

The lion stops and looks the man in the face. It shakes its tangled mane. The man stretches out a hand and rubs its golden nose. The lion steps forward and pushes him playfully in the chest with its nose. Then it rolls onto its back.

The man leans forward and strokes its belly.

"What's this?" Nero screams. "That lion is our best. It's eaten thirty men or more."

"The Christian used to be its keeper – it remembers his kindness."

"Kindness? In the arena? The mob have not come here to see kindness," the emperor raged.

But the mob is smiling. Nero turns to them. "Shall I have the gladiators kill them both?" he asks. The crowd grumbles then one voice calls back, "Spare them!"

Other voices join the cries. "Spare the Christian! Spare the lion! Spare them both!"

And Nero fears the mob. "I have decided … as your emperor," he cries, "to spare the Christian and the lion."

The crowd roars. "They love me," Nero smiles.

The lion rises to its feet. The gate is opened. The lion walks out of the arena. The man's arm is around its neck.

"Even in a place of death and horror there can be love," the man says.

The guard hears him and nods.

19

Volcano Cake

In AD 79 Mount Vesuvius erupted. 20,000 people died.
The Roman emperor of the time, Titus, was a greedy guts. Now, like
him, you can admire the eruption of Vesuvius – and pig out afterwards!

You will need:
3 sponge cakes
230g of soft
unsalted butter
300g icing sugar
4 big tablespoons
of drinking chocolate powder
4 tablespoons of milk
250g desiccated coconut
3 teaspoons of
green food colouring
Strawberry laces
Fizzy strip sweets
Jellybeans

I'M BAKING!

GREAT – YOU CAN MAKE ME A CAKE!

POMPEII

1 Place the three sponge cakes on top of each other. With a knife, trim off the edges of each cake – cutting into the top cake the most – until you have made a mountain shape. Keep the off-cuts of sponge.

2 Put the butter, the icing sugar, drinking chocolate powder and milk in a bowl and mix until smooth. There, you've just made butter icing. Yum! (Don't eat it all ... just yet. Or you'll be the one who's erupting.)

3 Using dollops of the butter icing as glue, stick some of the sponge off-cuts to the top of your Vesuvius. The idea is to make a rough, raised circle which will be the crater (the hole the lava bubbles come out).

20

4 Starting at the bottom, spread the gooey butter icing over the whole cake. Leave the top till last to allow the off-cuts time to set. Slap on extra icing around the joins between the cakes. Leave the cake to set for 30 minutes.

5 To make the grass, mix up the desiccated coconut with the green food colouring in a bowl. Spoon the 'grass' around the volcano cake.

6 Now for the really fun bit! (Readers who do NOT have a sweet tooth should look away.) Droop strawberry laces and fizzy strip sweets down from the crater so that it looks as if they are they erupting from the volcano's mouth. Add some droplets of lava using jellybeans. Any leftover cake pieces can be used to create a few volcanic boulders. Enjoy your sweet taste explosion!

A Horrible Hun...

Meet the trouble-making terror who drove the Romans round the bend –
and then met with a very bloody end...

Poisonous Profile

Name: Attila the Hun

Born: AD 403, somewhere in Asia.

Dad: King Munsdak of the Huns.

Died: AD 453 after a party.

Attila was the last and most powerful king of the horrible Huns. The Huns were barbarians – a brutal bunch of tribes that lived beyond the borders of the ever-so-snooty Roman Empire. They were a rough lot who liked nothing better then giving their fancy-pants Roman neighbours a bit of a bashing. But when it came to fierce, the Huns knocked spots off the rest and Attila was the horriblest Hun of 'em all. His hobby was catching bears and wolves and tearing their guts out – nice!

Li'l Attila

Attila had a rotten time when he was little. He was sent away as a hostage to Rome by an awful uncle. While he was there, he learned about the Roman army and made a plan to rule the world. (He was 'Hun-gry' for power!)

Hun number one

Attila was grown up by the time he got home. He was soon the top Hun. Those who didn't want Attila to be boss ended up dead. During Attila's cruel rule, the Huns' empire grew and grew and became the biggest in Europe. By this time the Roman Empire had been divided into two.

Anything for a lady...

Although he probably didn't need one, Attila's excuse for invading the Western Roman Empire was that he was claiming what was rightfully his. He claimed that he was engaged to the emperor's sister (she had only asked him for a favour!) and that the empire was his wedding gift! He didn't get married but he did smash his 'gift' to smithereens!

A bride too far!

Attila had 300 wives so you'd think he'd know how to survive a wedding party. Well, he didn't. When he fell into bed after the party he had a bad nosebleed. He was so drunk that he didn't even notice. Attila the Killer choked to death on his own blood!

22

...and some horrible fun

Warrior or Worrier?

Take this test to see if you've got what it takes to be a horrible Hun – a killer like Attila! Give yourself one point for every 'a' you answer, two points for every 'b', and three points for every 'c'. Answers on page 76.

1. What is your favourite drink?
a) Tea
b) Anything fizzy
c) Fermented horse milk

2. Where do you eat?
a) At the dinner table
b) In front of the TV
c) On horseback

3. What do you like to eat?
a) Salad
b) Chicken tikka
c) Raw meat that has been sat on all day

4. How often do you bathe?
a) Once or more a day
b) Once a month
c) What's a 'bath'?

Barbarian Hunt

Spot the seven beastly barbarian tribes listed below. The eighth is not a tribe but one of the oldest civilisations. Which one is it?

F	O	U	R	K	I	A	K	W	E
R	D	S	E	T	F	N	L	J	A
L	H	I	T	C	A	Y	H	A	B
P	O	D	B	R	L	T	N	P	N
Q	S	E	F	L	O	P	P	Y	S
H	U	N	R	G	M	G	T	T	Q
I	E	G	I	J	B	L	O	Y	X
A	B	S	D	Z	A	B	N	T	N
V	I	F	G	G	R	E	E	K	H
V	H	O	T	H	D	L	S	T	M

VISIGOTH   SUEBI   FRANK
OSTROGOTH   ALAN   HUN
LOMBARD   GREEK

Vile Vacation

Your tribe are on their way south to loot Rome and escape the Huns. Can you help them get there without running into Huns, Roman legions or stormy waters?

- HOME

- ROME

23

Big Bad Bill

Meet the foul fellow who branched out from France, made England his own and then ... sort of fell to pieces!

Of all the Normans, William, Duke of Normandy (1028-1087) has to be the most famous. He's known to the world as William the Conqueror.

Bill became Duke of Normandy at the age of seven and had a scary childhood, as he was always in danger of being murdered by people who wanted his land. He grew up tough enough to become a king – which he did when he conquered England.

The disappearing conqueror

After his death, Bill's body was buried in a cathedral in Normandy. By then he was more like William the Pong-queror. The burial didn't go well…

Funeral foul-up no. 1 The journey to the church was delayed by a fire in the town. Bill's burial procession was halted until the fire was put out!

Funeral foul-up no. 2 The undertakers crammed Bill's body into a small coffin and bits fell off.

Funeral foul-up no. 3 The smell of Bill's rotting body bits was so disgusting that the bishop rushed through the service – then everyone ran for it!

ANDMAYYOURSOULENTER THEGLORIOUSKINGDOMOFHEAVEN ANDRECEIVETHEMERCIFUL BLESSINGOFOURMOSTHOLY FATHERAMENRIGHTI'MOFF!

Bill's body never got to rest in peace.

In 1562, Protestants raided the cathedral, opened tombs and scattered skeletons. All that was left of Bill was his thigh bone. That was re-buried and a monument was built… but in 1792 a revolutionary mob demolished it!

A simple slab now marks where Bill was buried. But what happened to William the Conqueror's thigh bone? Some say the rioters threw it out – some say it's still there.

Perhaps someone should get digging and find out for themselves…

OVER MY DEAD BODY!

BILL ABANDONED

HORRIBLE HAPPENINGS

Bill met his awful end in France. The French king had made some nasty remarks about William being too fat. Billy went ballistic. "I'll set the whole of France ablaze," Big Bill threatened. He started by setting fire to the castle in a town called Mantes. William's horse stepped on a hot cinder and stumbled. The Conqueror fell forward onto the point of his saddle and did himself a nasty injury – probably burst his bladder. He died five weeks later in agony.

Horrid Hastings

In 1066, King Harold tried to see off William's nasty Normans.
But he and his army got more than an eyeful...

Meet the Mongols

Meanwhile in central Asia, a wild, wandering people called the Mongols were causing mayhem. Their cruel kings – 'khans' – were really 'khan-do' kind of guys!

GENGHIS KHAN

His idea of fun:
In a word ... conquest. He terrified his foes not only with ruthless slaughter but with maths – the Mongols spread the use of the abacus wherever they went.

Also known as:
Temujin. That was his name when he was young. When he became boss of all the nomad tribes in 1206, his people called him Genghis Khan, which means 'universal ruler'. They weren't far wrong – he came closer than anyone else to conquering the entire known world.

Harsh upbringing

But Genghis wasn't always such a tough guy. When he was a little boy, he was terrified of dogs. He had to toughen up fast, though. When he was about nine, his dad died, and his tribe deserted his family. They managed to survive by hunting rats and birds. A tiny roasted lark was a special 'tweet'.

They also had to dodge dangerous enemies who would take them prisoner – or worse. Once, Temujin was captured by an enemy tribe who planned to turn him into a slave. They tied his arms and neck to a wooden frame (called a 'yoke') to stop him getting away. But Tem bashed his guard over the head with the yoke. (You could even say the yoke was on him.) Then he escaped by hiding in a wagon-load of wool. (Bet his captors felt a bit sheepish.)

Foul Facts

After Genghis Khan captured one city, his soldiers started to slaughter all the survivors. One woman said to a soldier, "Spare my life and I will give you a great pearl!" When the soldier asked where the pearl was, the woman said she had swallowed it. So the soldier cut open the woman's stomach – and found the pearl inside. After hearing about this, grim Genghis gave the order that ALL the prisoners should have their stomachs cut open to see if they had done the same thing.

IT'S MONGREL VS. MONGOL!

TIMUR THE LAME

His idea of fun: Conquering, killing and destroying. The meanest of the marauding Mongols, Timur was even more brutal than Genghis Khan. He took over the trading city of Samarkand and used it as a base to wage a 40-year reign of terror against his neighbours.

Also known as: Tamerlane, Timur Lenk, Tamberlaine. His cruel 'lame' nickname caught on because he was said to have had a withered arm and leg.

High-rise horror

Timur liked building mosques (Muslim places of worship). But his favourite style of architecture was more horrid high-rise than holy house… he liked building towers of skulls. Here are some of his 'skullscraper' records:

 At Isfahan, he slaughtered 70,000 people to make his 'skullptures'.

 At Delhi, he gave 80,000 Indian enemies the axe.

At Delhi, he gave 80,000 Indian enemies the axe.

But he beat both beastly beheading records in Baghdad… with a pyramid of 90,000 decapitated heads.

All in all, hundreds of thousands of people died so that Timur could build his terrifying victory monuments.

Tall Timur tales

Sometimes folk tales tell you as much about a person as their true history. Here are couple about Timur – decide for yourself…

Sorry Sultan

In 1402 Timur captured the Ottoman Turk sultan Bayezid. It was said that he kept him in a cage and displayed him like an animal in a zoo.

A hard lesson

Tim's invading army had run out of water. They captured a shepherd boy, but he wouldn't tell them where he watered his sheep. So Tim began to beat him up – bash, bash, until his fists hurt. Tim pulled the boy's hood back – and found the boy had turned to stone! This statue wasn't speaking, so the army had to beat a retreat instead.

Secret Skull Stash

A pile of skulls always put a smile on the face of twisted Timur the Lame – now YOU can have a bone-headed buddy to cheer you up! This skull has a compartment to hide secret stuff in, too!

IT'S THE PERFECT PLACE TO HIDE MY FAVOURITE JELLY BEANS. SKULL–FUL!

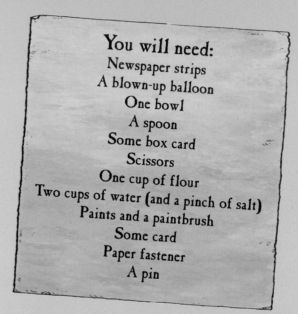

You will need:
Newspaper strips
A blown-up balloon
One bowl
A spoon
Some box card
Scissors
One cup of flour
Two cups of water (and a pinch of salt)
Paints and a paintbrush
Some card
Paper fastener
A pin

1 Mix the flour and water in a bowl until it's gloopy like glue. Stir well to get rid of any lumps. (TOP TIP: add a pinch of salt to stop your head going mouldy!) Dip the newspaper strips in the bowl and cover the balloon in one layer. Repeat this three times, letting each layer of newspaper dry before adding the next.

2 Make the shapes of the eye sockets with small rolls of gluey newspaper. Do the same to create the shape of the nose, and glue on some more small rolls of gluey, gooey paper to make some jagged, ugly teeth. Leave to dry. Then pop the balloon inside with a pin.

Top Tip
Use a bin liner as a work surface. Makes cleaning up easy!

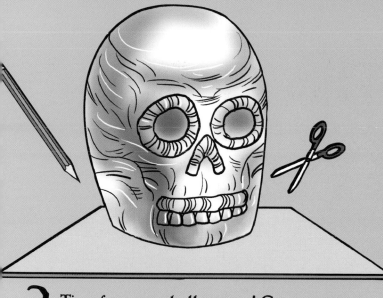

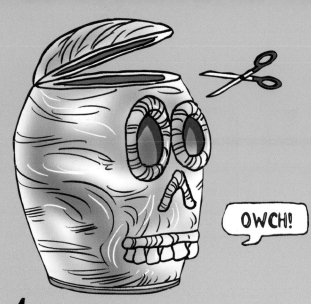

OWCH!

3 Time for some skull surgery! Get a grown-up to use a sharp knife to make a hole in the skull below the 'jaw'. Using this hole as a starting point, carefully cut off the bottom of the skull – just below the teeth – using scissors. Plop the chopped skull on a piece of card, trace around the base, and then cut out the circle. Tape it to the bottom and add a few more gluey paper strips to keep it in place.

4 Using the same 'hole-then-scissors' skull skill you learned in step 3, cut off the top of the skull. CAREFUL: you MUST make sure you leave a bit attached at the back. This will be the hinge that lets you flip the skull open and shut.

5 Now it's time to make your Skull Stash as grim and ghoulish as you wish. Paint it a beastly bone colour, maybe with yellow for the teeth and black for the eye sockets. When the paint is dry, use a pencil to draw on cracks (where it was whacked by Timur!) and shade in areas of decay. No one will touch your stash now!

Paint

... and now for some Mongol mind-benders!

SKULL SEARCH

Timur the Lame has been busy hiding eight skulls around this Mongol village. Can you spot them all? Answers on page 76.

In-tents Punishments

Mess with the khan's tent and you might peg it. But can you match the crime with the right punishment?

If you...

1) Sneaked up to the khan's tent without permission

2) Ran away after getting too close to the khan's tent

3) Entered the khan's tent without permission

Your punishment was to be...

a) Shot at with special blunt-tipped arrows

b) Beaten to a pulp

c) Executed – you axed for it!

Reign of Pain

Meet the cruel rulers who turned up the heat in Spain and the evil Inquisition that was about as popular as being prodded with a red-hot poker!

Gruesome twosome

After Isa married Ferdie, they joined their kingdoms together and made Spain one of the top nations in Europe.

While Ferdie was loopy for loot, Isabella was potty about praying. She wanted all of her subjects to follow her religion and be as religious as her. She ordered all Jewish people and Muslims to become Catholics – or get out. And she used the terrible Inquisition to punish anyone who wasn't Catholic enough for her liking. It was a reign of pain in Spain.

Ferdie was more than happy with Isabella's evil Inquisition. It gave him the perfect excuse to crush his enemies and nab their money. All in all, Ferdie and Isa turned out to be a perfectly monstrous match!

FERDINAND AND ISABELLA

This royal couple were a dastardly double act. Take greedy Ferdinand. He was king of Aragon (a part of northern Spain) but he still wanted more power and gold. That's why in 1469 he married Isabella – she was about to become queen of Castile (the kingdom next door). Isabella thought they were marrying for love. Altogether now – aaah!

Chris crosser

Ferdie was sneaky, too. When Christopher Columbus set out on a voyage, Ferdie promised the adventurer a big reward. But when Chris returned without any gold – foul Ferdie sent him packing with nothing!

DAFT DEEDS

It is said that Isabella vowed she would wear the same clothes until the Muslims in Spain were completely conquered. (So her smell was as bad as her attitude!) In 1492, three or four years later, her wish came true... so she could finally change her clothes. Pwoar!

MORE LIKE ISA – SMELLA!

Dungeon of Dread

Deep in the evil Inquisition's dark and dank dungeons, terrible tortures took place...

Heretics (people accused of not being good Catholics) were tortured. Sooner or later most of them confessed to something – even if they were innocent. And then, of course, the 'guilty' ones were punished. They just couldn't win!

CONFESS, HERETIC!

OK, I CONFESS! BUT WHAT SHOULD I CONFESS TO?

YOU CAN TAKE YOUR DRINK CAN'T YOU, EH?

Torturers really put their woodwork skills to the test as they invented ever more horrible ways of inflicting pain. Nobody wanted to take a turn on this wheel of misfortune.

Water torture was stomach-splittingly sick. Water was poured into a victim's mouth so they had to swallow it – or drown. They really had a belly-full!

For this stretching torture, the victim was tied between a weight and a pulley. When the rope was pulled – the victim was stretched!
OH, PULL THE OTHER ONE!!
Imagine how awful it must have been to have to wait, knowing the agonies you were going to have to suffer…
OH, YOU PULLEY BULLY! HE'S IN FOR A LONG STRETCH!
DON'T WORRY ABOUT ME, THERE'S NO RUSH, TAKE YOUR TIME
YEAH, I SHOULD BE IN THE HAUL OF FAME!
The torturers used red-hot pincers. They were heated so that they burnt the victims' wounds shut as soon they made them. This was because the torturers weren't allowed to shed any blood. How thoughtful.
The torturers wore hoods so that they wouldn't be recognized. It also made them extra scary.

Tricky Dicky

This crafty character was only king for two years, but he made quite an awful impression...

Richard III was ruthless and rotten. In a play about the king, William Shakespeare said that Richard (a) killed Henry VI – the previous king, (b) killed Henry's son Edward, (c) drowned his own brother George in a barrel of wine and (d) suffocated his nephews in the Tower of London. Tricky Dicky must have been busy, but the death of this sorry lot did leave the crown of England up for grabs – by Richard!

Shakespeare may have fibbed a bit to make his play more exciting, but Dirty Dick was certainly hard-hearted. He once refused to finish supper until a lord's head had been cut off!

Ditched and dumped

Richard III's reign only lasted two years. He was killed at the Battle of Bosworth Field. The misery didn't end there. His body was paraded, naked and filthy, through the streets. It was buried in an unmarked grave, in Leicester.

Poisonous Profile ☠ ☠

Name: Richard Plantagenet

Born: 1452

Reigned: 1483-85

Died: 1485 at the battle of Bosworth Field. He was the last king from the House of York and the last English king to die in battle.

LET ME GIVE YOU A HAND, YOUR MAJESTY! YOUNG EDWARD WAS JUST 12 YEARS OLD WHEN HE WAS SMOTHERED. SO HIS HEAD WOULD HAVE BEEN A BIT SMALL FOR THE CROWN ANYWAY

DID YOU KNOW...?

There are lots of stories about where Richard's body ended up. Some say that his burial site now lies under a car park in the city of Leicester.

LONG STAY CAR PARK

THIS ISN'T A SPEED HUMP, YOU KNOW!

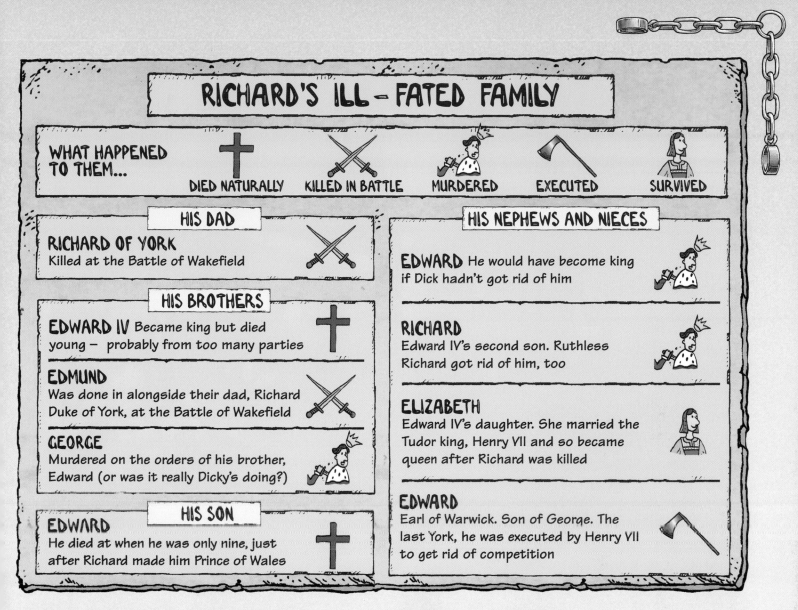

RICHARD'S ILL-FATED FAMILY

WHAT HAPPENED TO THEM...

✝ DIED NATURALLY ⚔ KILLED IN BATTLE 👑 MURDERED 🪓 EXECUTED 🧍 SURVIVED

HIS DAD

RICHARD OF YORK
Killed at the Battle of Wakefield ⚔

HIS BROTHERS

EDWARD IV Became king but died young – probably from too many parties ✝

EDMUND
Was done in alongside their dad, Richard Duke of York, at the Battle of Wakefield ⚔

GEORGE
Murdered on the orders of his brother, Edward (or was it really Dicky's doing?) 👑

HIS SON

EDWARD
He died at when he was only nine, just after Richard made him Prince of Wales ✝

HIS NEPHEWS AND NIECES

EDWARD He would have become king if Dick hadn't got rid of him 👑

RICHARD
Edward IV's second son. Ruthless Richard got rid of him, too 👑

ELIZABETH
Edward IV's daughter. She married the Tudor king, Henry VII and so became queen after Richard was killed 🧍

EDWARD
Earl of Warwick. Son of George. The last York, he was executed by Henry VII to get rid of competition 🪓

Tudor truth or Tudor tale?

These days we're smart enough to know that the way your body looks doesn't mean much about the way you are inside. But that's not the way the Tudors saw it – particularly as dodgy Dicky's family and their's had been at loggerheads for years. Here are some daft things they said...

He was a bizarre baby. Richard spent two years in his mum's tum and was born with long hair and teeth!

HE REALLY WAS BORN YESTERDAY

WHY PICK ON ME?

He had a withered arm. But Richard was well known for being a savage warrior. Could he have fought so well with just one good arm? What do you think?

IT'S A LUNCHPACK, NOT A HUNCHBACK

Richard was a hunchback. Turns out the Tudors painted a hump onto Richard's portrait long after he was dead.

37

Tower of Power

Like many cruel royals before him, Richard III used the terrifying Tower of London to do away with his enemies and rivals.

DON'T BE SO HASTY!

After one of Richard's main enemies, Lord Hastings, was arrested, Richard begged the Royal Council to have him executed. Richard got his way!

One tower echoed with strange cries and roars – but they weren't the groans of prisoners. They were animal noises – because this was the Lion Tower where the royal zoo was kept.

STILL, IT'S SAFER THAN WORKING WITH RICHARD

While Richard's brother, Edward IV was king, another brother, George, was plotting treason. Ed found out and had George executed in the Bowyer Tower. Some say George was drowned in a barrel of his favourite wine – and that Richard did it.

In 1471, men armed with daggers leapt into the Wakefield Tower and stabbed the man inside while he was praying. The victim was King Henry VI, who was a prisoner of Edward IV and his brother Richard.

SAY YOUR PRAYERS, HENRY!

THIS'LL CUSHION THE BLOW

WE'RE MAKING A MINT

The Royal Mint, where coins were made, was in the Tower. Sensible really, as it was one of the strongest places in the kingdom.

The Bloody Tower was where, it's said, Richard had his two nephews bumped off. No one knows exactly what happened but the princes were probably smothered.

HIC!

Beastly Bosworth Field

When Richard III's army of Yorks met the
Lancasters of Henry Tudor, the scene was set
for blood and bitter betrayal ...

Fierce Field Day

1. Richard's army outnumbered Henry's, but Richard got let down by some of his so-called 'friends', such as the Earl of Northumberland. Northumberland and his men refused to fight …
2. … then another of Richard's pals, Lord Stanley, changed sides – and attacked Richard's men from behind!
3. Soldiers took the chance to grab armour and weapons from dead enemies. The gear could be sold later. So they killed – then made a killing!
4. The fighting was brutal and bloody. Armoured knights were tough nuts to crack. The best way to kill them was to knock them over – then stab them in the eye. Ouch.
5. Richard III may have been a bully, but he was no coward! When he saw he was betrayed, he led a charge against Henry Tudor. He speared Henry's flag carrier and chopped down Henry's giant bodyguard. But then Henry's knights surrounded Richard and cut him down.
6. Winner: Henry Tudor!

Henry's Horrid Highlights

From handsome young party animal to hated headchopper, Henry VIII certainly made his mark, creating the Church of England and ransacking the monasteries along the way...

Henry's Kids (and what became of them)

Edward VI
King of England (1547 to 1553)
At nine, young Ed was too young to rule so he had helpers. He was engaged to Mary Queen of Scots, but this fell through. (She was a Catholic and he was a Protestant so there would have been big problems.) Ed was a sickly lad and died at the age of 16. He named his cousin Lady Jane Grey as his successor because she was a Protestant.

Mary I
Queen of England (1553 to 1558)
After nine days, Ed's sister pushed Jane off the throne and pushed her head on the block. CHOP! A devout Catholic, Mary made the Pope head of the English church again. She married King Philip of Spain (also a Catholic) who helped her lose Calais (in France) to the French people. Unpopular and a little bonkers, she became known as 'Bloody Mary'.

Elizabeth I
Queen of England (1558 to 1603)
Elizabeth pretended to be a Catholic while her sister Mary was Queen. But when it was her turn for the throne it was ALL CHANGE – Protestants IN and Catholics OUT. Mary Queen of Scots got the chop because she was a Catholic and some people wanted her as queen. Elizabeth never married but had a soft spot for the Earl of Essex. However, this didn't stop her from having his head chopped off as well!

Traitor Toppers

You betrayed Henry VIII at your peril – he loved displaying traitors' heads on sticks! Here's how to have your very own head collection.

You will need:
Newspaper or rags
An unwanted pair of tights
Rubber band
Wool hair
Paints and a paintbrush
Black pen
Pencils
Glue
Cardboard box

1 Carefully cut off one foot from an old pair of tights and stuff it with scrunched-up newspaper or some rags. When it's really stuffed, close off the end of the tights by slipping a rubber band around it. (Maybe get a grown-up to help with this bit.)

2 Push your favourite pencil through the rubber band 'neck' until it's deep inside the 'head'.

3 Using the pencil as a holder, give the head a good thick coat of sickly light green paint. Leave to dry. (It might take a while. Boring!)

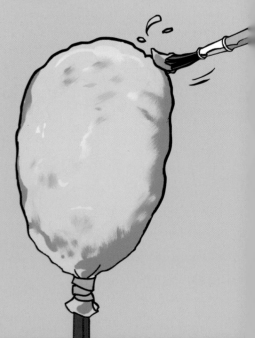

4 Once dry, use marker pens and pencils to draw on any foul facial features you desire. Come on, get gruesome!

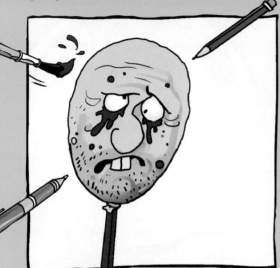

5 Make some lifeless hair from the wool and glue it in place. You can also glue some strands of red wool to the bottom to be horrible veins hanging down limply from the neck. Right, now make some more! Chop, chop.

Top Tip
Why not make a Traitors' Gate to keep your pens in? Cut the top of a box into a battlement then paint the outside. Give those heads a home!

47

Tucking in with ...

Royal banquets were real gross-outs, piled high with weird and wonderful food, while the poor got by on rotten meat and turnips ...

Live birds were stuffed into pies so that they flew out when the crust was cut. Hot droppings in pastry anyone?

Roast monster? Nope, it's the front half of a cockerel stitched to the back of a pig – a dish known as a cockatrice.

Eye eye! Peacocks would be skinned before being roasted. They were then stuffed back into their skin and decorated with feathers.

Wine was the drink of the day – a far safer bet than water. Sack, a kind of rough sherry, was also popular – they drank it like fish!

About 20 different types of jelly would be on the menu for the rich. Castle and animal shapes were their favourite! Henry VIII loved them.

No, that's not a plate of guts! This knotty pile is a plate of 'jumbles' – crunchy, doughy biscuits, flavoured with cinnamon or aniseed.

the Tudors

Among the nobility, it was considered jolly good fun to 'make a stink while you drink'.

Catching a rabbit was one way the poor could get meat. The bunny was left hanging around for a while, so herbs and spices were used to disguise the taste of rotting flesh!

Pewter plates were only for the posh. Most people ate off 'trenchers'– slabs of wood or bread.

A cheaper meal would be a bowl of 'sops' – hunks of stale bread soaking in a bowl of fatty gravy.

This dog's got a fight on its paws. Meat was a rare treat for the poor, who made do with turnips, beans or cabbage most of the time.

Bloody Mary

Mean, moody and not very magnificent, Mary Tudor was queen for only a few years – but that was long enough for her to earn her gory nickname.

☠ Poisonous Profile ☠

Name: Mary Tudor

Born: February 18, 1516

Mum and dad: Horrible Henry VIII and Catherine of Aragon. (Henry divorced Catherine to marry Anne Boleyn. When little Mary tried to fight for her mum, Henry VIII had her shut up in some horrible houses)

Brothers and sisters: Edward (who ruled first), Elizabeth (who would rule after Mary)

Died: November 17, 1558

Misery Mary was so mad about being a Catholic that she had Protestants (members of the Church of England set up by her dad) burned at the stake if they didn't follow her religion.

But that wasn't the only thing Mary did that got up people's noses. One of her daftest deeds was to marry the future king of Spain. This made the people of England very cross indeed.

A sourpuss and sickly, Mary went down in history known as 'Bloody Mary'.

DID YOU KNOW…?

Mary was the first woman to be crowned Queen of England. (OK, there had been an Empress Matilda, who had fought to rule England 400 years before, but she had never been crowned.)

Beastly brother

Before Henry VIII snuffed it, he said Mary could be Queen if Edward died without children. Easy. Of course, history is never as simple as that. Edward did die without any kids, but while he was dying he hatched a plan with his chief minister to keep England Protestant. He named Lady Jane Grey (a Protestant) as his successor, not his sister Mary (a Catholic).

But Mary wasn't having any of that. She knew the English would not be happy with a Catholic queen, so she hatched her own plan. She told everyone that the country would stay Protestant. It worked. The people hadn't learned the lesson – 'NEVER TRUST A TUDOR'!

Her Hunky Hubby

Mary fancied Phil, but Phil didn't fancy Mary... and that made her murderously miserable.

PHILIP II OF SPAIN

Philip was a big hit with Queen Mary ... but not with her people. Marrying Philip was a big mistake. The English didn't like him because he was Spanish and he was a Catholic ... and Spanish Catholics were 'saving' the souls of thousands of people who were not Catholic by torturing them and burning their bodies.

> THIS IS A LIE. THE CATHOLIC CHURCH DID NOT BURN A SINGLE PERSON TO DEATH
>
> YES DEAR

What happened was the Church found the victims guilty and handed them over to the government ... who then burned them. So Philip was right – the Catholic Church didn't actually burn a single person. they just sent them to their deaths. Phil brought this charming hobby to England.

Mary loved Phil madly, but Phil was never quite so keen.

What did Philip do straight after the wedding?

> I'M OFF TO FLANDERS TO FIGHT FOR SPAIN. I'LL BE BACK IN SIX WEEKS

He lied. He came a year later for a short stay then left for good. Mary was very miserable. She decided that she must have upset God. So, to make God happy, she burned more Protestants.

Mary wanted Phil back so badly that she sent his favourite pies across to Flanders. "The way to a man's heart is through his stomach," they used to say. But the pies didn't do the trick – he never came back!

> GREAT PIES, AND I DON'T HAVE TO LIVE WITH MARY!

Much later, when Mary lay dying, England and France were at war. (Her hubby Philip's Spain had gone to war with France so Mary's England had to join in – whether they liked it or not.)

When the peace treaty was brought to Mary for her to sign, she was too ill to read it. The documents stayed by her bedside. When she died the next day, the papers had vanished. Mary's ministers searched the room and questioned Mary's chief lady-in-waiting.

Minister: "Have you seen any long rolls of parchment?"

Lady: "Long rolls of parchment? Oh yes. They were so useful I used them all up."

Minister: "Used them for what?"

Lady: "Why, to wrap up the Queen's corpse!"

DAFT DEEDS

> S'POSE IT WAS MORE OF A REST-IN-PEACE TREATY

The Sizzling Stake

A dry moat beside a college in Oxford was the unlikely site of some of Mary's most hot and horrific acts. Three bishops got baked here on the orders of the mean queen herself.

CHILLY IN YOUR UNDIES, SIR? YOU'LL BE NICE 'N' TOASTY SOON...

HOW MUCH WO SIR LIKE?

YOWCH!

Important nobles had the front row seats for each bishop bonfire. How's that for a seat beside an open fire?

Local traders took advantage of the gory gathering by setting up stalls to sell Tudor chews. (Cooking outdoors always makes people peckish!)

Hundreds crowded round to see the bishops burn. The crowd admired the ones who kept their 'cool' in the fire!

Archbishop Thomas Cranmer got turned into charcoal in Oxford. Cranmer is supposed to have stripped to his undies and walked to the stake bravely.

Spanish friars called on Cranmer to give up being a Protestant at the last minute – but he wouldn't.

Preachers loudly encouraged people to be Catholics. Perhaps they were worried they'd be next on the fire.

OOOF!

Big bullying soldiers held back the eager crowds.

Some people used the burnings as a good excuse for a sneaky bit of Protestant bashing!

HONEST, IT'S THE OFFER OF A LIFETIME

The burnings didn't stop people being Protestants – in fact, it made some more determined. But if they wanted to buy a banned book here they had to be very careful.

Flaming Hell...

Do you go barmy for bonfires? Are you batty for barbecues? Well, then you're a lot like Misery Mary – except she liked her fires to have Protestants on top!

Flaming Mary

Some modern historians think Mary has been treated unfairly in history books. "She wasn't all that bad," they say. In terms of executing people, her father Henry VIII and sister Elizabeth I were both worse. But when it came to horrible burnings, she was the top Tudor:

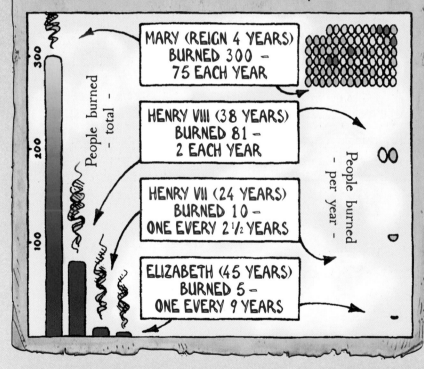

People burned – total –

People burned – per year –

MARY (REIGN 4 YEARS)
BURNED 300 –
75 EACH YEAR

HENRY VIII (38 YEARS)
BURNED 81 –
2 EACH YEAR

HENRY VII (24 YEARS)
BURNED 10 –
ONE EVERY 2½ YEARS

ELIZABETH (45 YEARS)
BURNED 5 –
ONE EVERY 9 YEARS

Bloody Mary, they say, was quite mad, And the nastiest taste that she had Was for Protestant burning – Seems she had a yearning To kill even more than her dad.

Repent AND Die

Mary believed that people who didn't follow the Catholic ways would roast in the fires of hell. The best way to make them say 'sorry' was to stick them on a bonfire – once they had a feel for hell-fire they would repent.

The fire would not be put out of course. They would die whether they said sorry or not! But at least Mary felt sure they would go to heaven and the pain would be worthwhile.

The law said that Mary had to sign every death warrant. She must have had writer's cramp because there were a 'helluva' lot – 240 men and 60 women.

DID YOU KNOW...?

Lots of murdering monarchs said sorry for their dastardly deeds when they died – but not Mary. She only stopped burning people when she snuffed it herself. And on the day of her death she managed to sign two last orders for burnings!

more puzzles!

Misery Mary's Maze
A bishop stands accused of being a Protestant. Can you help him to avoid being burned at the stake?

Misery Mary Brainteaser
Mug up on your Mary knowledge with this quick quiz. Answers on page 77.

1. When Mary became queen, the citizens of London were happy. How did they celebrate? Did they ...
a) throw money out of the windows
b) sing and dance in the streets
c) fill up fountains with wine

2. Later, Misery Mary wasn't quite so popular and ended up with the nickname 'Bloody Mary'. How did she earn such a nice name? Was it because...
a) the Tudors were terrible swearers and couldn't help calling her 'Bloody' or even 'Flaming Mary'?
b) she enjoyed regular burnings and beheadings of Protestants?
c) she loved drinking the cocktail (made with tomato juice) with that name?

3. When Misery Mary finally croaked, her chief lady-in-waiting was at hand to wrap up her corpse. What did Mary's body get wrapped up inside?
a) A binbag
b) A rug
c) A peace treaty

A Scary Supertsar

Russians often call their country 'Mother Russia'.
Well, here's one rotten Russian ruler who made his 'mother' absolutely miserable!

Poisonous Profile

Name: Ivan 'The Terrible' Rurik. (The Russians called him grozny, which means 'the Awesome'. This was translated as 'the Terrible' – and it stuck. Well, it suited him!)

Born: August 25, 1530

Mum and Dad: Vasily III and Yelena Glinskaya

Brothers or sisters: Little brother Yury.

IVAN THE TERRIBLE
RULED: 1533–1584

Ivan was a cruel and crazy ruler. When he was only 17 he decided to call himself 'Tsar of all the Russias'. Tsar is Russian for Caesar, and it was his way of claiming to be related to ancient emperors (fibber!).

He created a personal army of bullies, the Oprichniks, whose job it was to kill and torture anyone he didn't like the look of. And he didn't like the look of an awful lot of people!

Ivan's temper wasn't the only thing that was out of control. He also ate and drank far too much. He got fat, his guts started to rot, his skin peeled off and he really stank. He acted terrible, looked terrible and smelled terrible too.

Despite his endless killing and torturing, Ivan thought of himself as very 'holy' and loved praying. He turned one of his palaces into a monastery and made himself an abbot!

He chose 300 of his favourite Oprichniks and turned them into his monks. He spent mornings praying with these mean monks, and then after a nice meal and a nap he would pop down to the dungeons to watch prisoners being tortured by his faithful thugs. How 'holy' horrible.

DID YOU KNOW…?

Ivan loved English things – especially the Queen! Even though he already had a wife, Ivan once decided he had to marry Elizabeth I. Liz had no intention of marrying anyone, least of all a nutty Russian Tsar. She offered her grand niece instead. Gee thanks, great aunty!

IVAN'S ILL-FATED FAMILY

WHAT HAPPENED TO THEM...

DIED   BUMPED OFF   SENT AWAY   DROWNED   SURVIVED

HIS WOEFUL WIVES . . .

ANASTASIA
Ivan thought she was poisoned by his enemies †

MARIA
Ivan got bored with her, so he bumped her off

MARFA
Died 16 days after marrying Ivan †

ANNA
Ivan sent her to a convent ☞

ANNA
Anna-nother one bites the dust! †

VASSILISSA
Ivan caught her flirting, so he impaled her boyfriend on a stake and sent her to a convent ☞

MARIA (another one)
Just after marrying her he found out she'd already had a boyfriend, so he drowned her the very next day

MARIA (yes, another one!)
The lucky one – she outlived him

...AND THREE OF HIS CURSED KIDS

LITTLE DIMITRI
He was taken on a long trip with his dad, caught a cold and died suddenly. (Some say his dastardly dad drowned him)

IVAN
He shared the Tsar's taste for blood and loved joining him on weekend massacres. But dad bashed his head in during a row

FEODOR
Became Tsar after Ivan died. A bit odd all round. He preferred bell-ringing and playing with clowns to being Tsar

How to survive dinner with Ivan

• **Don't scream – even if he pours boiling hot soup over your head**

At one of his dreadful dinners, Ivan was irritated by a prince called Gvozdev. He poured a bowl of boiling hot soup over Gvozdev's head. When the prince screamed in pain, Ivan stuck a knife in his chest. He then called a doctor, saying "I have jested a little too roughly with him." And the doctor replied: "So roughly that only God can bring him back to life. He is no longer breathing."

I WAS LUCKY – THE SOUP WAS COLD

WELL, EAR TODAY, GONE TOMORROW

• **Don't complain – even if he chops bits off you**

Ivan once cut off the ear of one of his dinner guests, Boris Titov, as a joke. Because he didn't want to make a fuss that would upset the tetchy Tsar even more, Mr Titov didn't even change his expression!

In 1570, Ivan the Terrible heard a rumour that the people of Novgorod were plotting against him, so he and his paid thugs – the Oprichniks – attacked the city. Weeks of death, terror and torture were to follow ...

Citizens got tied up and thrown into sledges, which were then pushed into the freezing cold river.

Awful Antifreeze

After weeks of bashing, blood and death, Ivan decided that the people of Novgorod weren't traitors after all and went home. Nobody knows for certain how many poor souls had been slaughtered, but it may have been as many as 60,000. The people of Novgorod said that Ivan's attack spilled so much blood into their river that it didn't freeze over in winter for years afterwards.

Novgorod WAS famous for its beautifully carved wooden houses. Sadly they caught fire easily.

The Oprichnik's own badge of terror was a broom and a dog's head. Some say they carried around real brooms and real dog's heads!

Ivan enjoyed cooking his victims, and often had them roasted, fried, baked or boiled!

Shocking Sultans

Meet the ruthless rulers who killed their kids, gutted their gardeners, shot arrows at slaves and worried their wives!

MEHMED II RULED: 1451–1481

This shocking sultan had a hooked nose and big red lips. People said he looked like a parrot about to eat a bowl of cherries! (Of course, they didn't say it to his face.)

Greatest deed: Capturing Constantinople. Turks and other Muslims had tried and failed to capture this huge Christian city for hundreds of years.

Rottenest act: When his cannons sunk an Italian ship, he cut the heads off all of the survivors – except the captain. He was impaled on a stake.

WHO'S A PRETTY BOY THEN?

Foul Facts

Mehmed II was mad about gardening. This green-fingered fellow's favourite homegrown harvest was his cucumbers. Think gardening is a peaceful pastime? Not for Mehmed. When a cucumber went missing, Mehmed went into a sultan-sized strop ... and had all of his gardeners' guts ripped open to see if one of them had eaten it.

I'VE ALWAYS SAID CUCUMBERS GIVE YOU INDIGESTION

OSMAN II RULED: 1618–1622

Greatest deed: Becoming sultan at the age of 13. But it all went downhill from there.

Rottenest act: Osman was just as 'orrible as his elders. He liked to practise archery – by using his pages (young servants) as targets.

Biggest mistake: Trying to take away the power of his top troops. They didn't like that at all. They captured Osman and rode him through the city on a lame horse to embarrass him. But it got much worse…

Sticky end: They strangled him and crushed his naughty bits! Then they cut off one of his ears and sent it to his mum.

HMM – THIS SULTAN JOB COULD BE MURDER!

Murad IV RULED: 1623–1640

Greatest deed: Murad didn't really do any great things – apart from being a great big barmy bully.

Biggest mistake: Becoming sultan when he was only five. Not that he could really help it. His mean mum bullied him into taking the job. She even let soldiers beat him up. No wonder Murad grew up bad.

Rottenest act: He liked to wander the streets in disguise with his executioner. Anybody who looked at him funnily or acted odd was executed on the spot! Once he ran through the streets hacking off the heads of men with fat necks – just for fun.

Sticky end: Unluckily for Murad (but lucky for everyone else) Murad died at the age of 27 from drinking too much.

DAFT DEEDS

Murad was a real misery guts. He didn't like people singing. Once, when he was out hunting, some women were singing while having a picnic. He ordered all the women to be drowned. On another occasion, he had his palace cannons sink a boat of women who had sailed too close to the walls.

> I HATE MODERN POP MUSIC

> THAT'S FUNNY – YOU'VE JUST HAD A HIT...

Biggest mistake: Ibrahim wasn't much interested in governing. He preferred partying.

Rottenest act: Having some of the women in his harem tied up in sacks and thrown into the sea.

Sticky end: Ibrahim became so mad that some of his soldiers decided to murder him.

Ibrahim RULED: 1640–1648

Ibrahim had been locked up in a building called the Cage since he was a kid. This was because his bad brother Murad didn't want him causing trouble. When Murad died, it was Ibrahim's turn to be sultan. He wouldn't leave the Cage until he had seen Murad's dead body.

Greatest deed: Ibrahim was really sweet on a great big woman he nicknamed 'Sugar Cube'. She reminded him of a cow he adored!

> I LOVE IT WHEN YOU'RE IN A ROMANTIC MOOO –D

Harem Hassle

Welcome to the harem: the posh prison where the Ottoman sultans kept their girlfriends. But watch your back – tricks and treachery are around every corner...

Most of the harem was a mind-bending maze of tiny dark rooms and twisting corridors. Once you were in, you might never get out...

Bad sultan Murad IV had a horrible hobby: dunking his harem girls in a deep pool of water – and shooting them with a peashooter when they came up for air!

I COULD MURDER A KEBAB...

MORE WINE, YOUR WONDERFULNESS?

I'M YOUR BIGGEST FAN...

WE NEED TO ACCELERATE OUR PLANS FOR POWER...

FULL THROTTLE, MY DEAR

The only men allowed into the harem – apart from the sultan – were 'eunuchs' (say *you-nucks*). A eunuch was a slave who'd had his dangly bits chopped off! They couldn't have girlfriends so the sultan trusted them to look after the place.

Harem girls who displeased the sultan got sewn into bags and thrown into the sea. Talk about getting the sack!

The sultan's mum and the chief eunuch were the most powerful people in the harem. By working together they could crush their rivals, get rich ... and even run the empire!

Handy Hand

The insultin' sultans were fond of chopping off the hands of criminals – but they never came up with any practical uses for all those off-cuts...

THAT'S HANDY

You will need:
Stiff card
Pencil
Newspaper
Drinks can
Vaseline
Kitchen towel
Masking tape
PVA glue and
a bowl of water
Acrylic paints
Paintbrush
Felt-tip pens

1 Place your hand palm up on some stiff card and draw around it. Cut it out carefully.

2 Turn over the hand and bend the thumb and fingers inwards a bit. Then, using masking tape, attach a few small pieces of rolled up newspaper to the wrist. These will be the severed veins and arteries.

3 Take a drinks can and rub a little Vaseline around its base. Plonk it squarely in the palm of the hand. Now mix some PVA glue with water in a bowl. Screw up some newspaper into small balls, dip them in the gluey gloop and then stick them around the can until they hold it in place. Wait for the balls to dry... then take away the can.

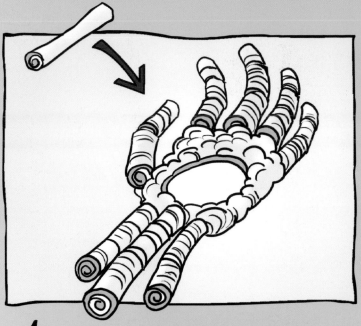

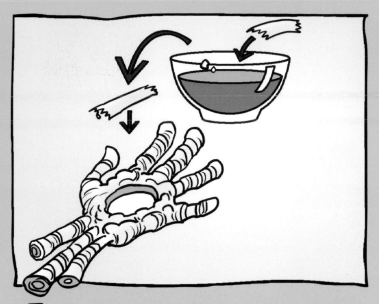

4 Take some more newspaper and roll it into sausage shapes. Tape these to the fingers. Then scrunch up some more newspaper and glue it into any 'empty areas'.

5 Right – time to give your hand a thick layer of clammy skin. Tear some kitchen roll into strips, dip them in the watery glue, then slip the strips on the hand until it is completely covered. Leave it to dry.

6 Okay – it's grisly decoration time. Paint the hand so it looks really, really gruesome. (Acrylic paints work best.) Make those severed bits and bones look gross. There you have it ... a sickening drinks holder – fit for a sultan!

Top Tip
It might be easier to add the really disgusting details with felt-tip pens once all the putrid paint is dry.

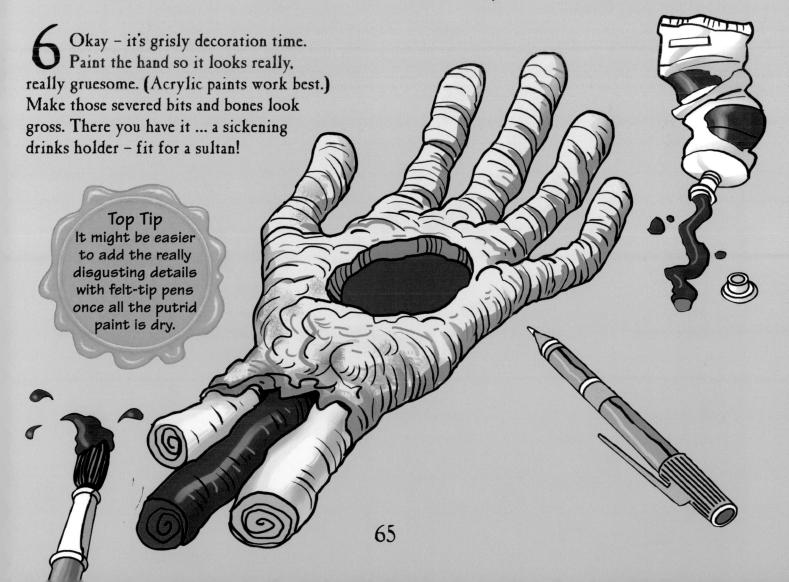

...a few Ottoman oddities!

Harem Scare 'em

Can you escape the harem without being nabbed by eunuchs, guards and a scary sultana?

ODD OTTOMAN

Eight characters from the Ottoman court are lurking in this wicked wordsearch. But which one was never an actual Ottoman?

MURAD			VLAD	
SULEIMAN			ROXELLANA	
IBRAHIM			MUSTAFA	
OSMAN			MEHMED	

W	E	M	U	S	T	A	F	A	I
X	P	V	B	S	G	U	N	O	B
Y	W	S	Q	S	R	A	D	M	R
V	M	I	U	D	L	U	S	H	A
L	B	J	T	L	P	M	L	C	H
A	P	L	E	S	E	W	F	M	I
D	U	X	S	W	I	I	O	U	M
T	O	S	M	A	N	E	M	R	D
R	I	Z	E	L	A	H	U	A	U
D	K	E	M	E	H	M	E	D	N

On the Ott Spot
Have a stab at this Ottoman quiz and see how many you get right!

1) Which drink was invented in the Ottoman Empire?
a) Coffee
b) Water
c) Lemonade

2) Who was the first ever Ottoman?
a) Wizard of Oz
b) Osman Gazi
c) Donny Osman

3) What did the mad sultan Murad IV ban?
a) Sultanas
b) Hair
c) Smoking

4) What animal decoration was worn by snazzy sultans and cool concubines?
a) Rabbit Droppings
b) Heron feathers

c) Horse shoes

5) Sultan Bayezid I was beaten by the mean Mongol ruler Timur the Lame. What did Timur do to the sultan?
a) He kept him in a cage like a bird
b) Became his best friend forever
c) Made him a cake

Unfair Empires

Here's what went on when Europeans with guns got greedy and went gallivanting around the globe. See what happens when Britannia waives the rules!

THE SPANISH REALLY GOT THE CRAZE FOR COLONIES GOING IN THE 1500s. THEY TOOK OVER MEXICO AND SOUTH AMERICA — AND TOOK PILES OF GOLD AND SILVER FROM THE INDIANS.

THE ENGLISH, FRENCH AND DUTCH STARTED THEIR OWN COLONIES IN THE AMERICAS. THESE WERE REALLY JUST BASES TO RAID SPANISH SHIPS FROM. BUT THEY DIDN'T SEE IT AS PIRACY — IT WAS JUST BUSINESS!

PIRATES!

NO, BUSINESSMEN — AND HERE'S MY CARD!

I'VE GOT MORE PIECES OF EIGHT THAN I KNOW WHAT TO DO WITH!

WE'RE IN THE MONEY!

HMM — I FANCY SOME OF THAT!

THE BRITS ALSO MADE MONEY BY GOING TO AFRICA AND TRADING GUNS AND GOLD FOR SLAVES. THEN THEY SOLD THE SLAVES IN AMERICA — FOR A FAT PROFIT!

THE SLAVE TRADE IS GREAT! THE AMERICANS GET SLAVES, WE GET RICH...

EVERYBODY WINS!

EXCEPT US

HAVING A COLONY WAS A GOOD WAY TO MAKE MONEY. PLUS IT WAS EASY TO TAKE OVER A PLACE WHEN THE INVADERS HAD GUNS — AND THE LOCALS DIDN'T.

HERE'S THE DEAL — YOU PAY US TAXES AND WE TAKE YOUR STUFF!

WE'RE HERE TO KEEP YOU COMPANY

BUSINESS AS USUAL, THEN

BOTH THE BRITS AND THE FRENCH WANTED TO HAVE COLONIES IN THE RICH LAND OF INDIA. THE BRITISH 'HONOURABLE EAST INDIA COMPANY' TOOK CONTROL OF MANY INDIAN KINGDOMS — USING GUNS OR TRICKS.

WHEN THE BRITS BEAT THE FRENCH IN THE SEVEN YEARS WAR, BRITAIN GOT TO KEEP THE FRENCH BITS OF INDIA AND NORTH AMERICA...

?

HELLO. THERE WAS A WAR IN EUROPE — AND WE WON YOU

Home in the Raj

The British government in India was called the 'Raj'.
In the Raj, the Brits were in charge! These rotten rulers bossed,
boozed and snoozed while the Indians did all the work ...

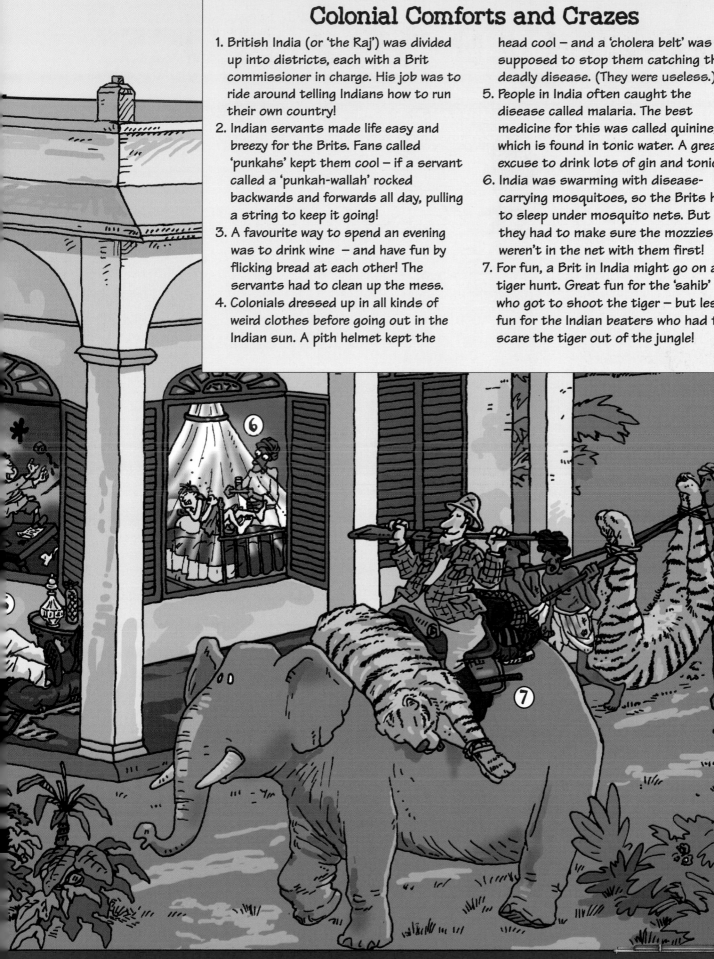

Colonial Comforts and Crazes

1. British India (or 'the Raj') was divided up into districts, each with a Brit commissioner in charge. His job was to ride around telling Indians how to run their own country!

2. Indian servants made life easy and breezy for the Brits. Fans called 'punkahs' kept them cool – if a servant called a 'punkah-wallah' rocked backwards and forwards all day, pulling a string to keep it going!

3. A favourite way to spend an evening was to drink wine – and have fun by flicking bread at each other! The servants had to clean up the mess.

4. Colonials dressed up in all kinds of weird clothes before going out in the Indian sun. A pith helmet kept the head cool – and a 'cholera belt' was supposed to stop them catching that deadly disease. (They were useless.)

5. People in India often caught the disease called malaria. The best medicine for this was called quinine, which is found in tonic water. A great excuse to drink lots of gin and tonic!

6. India was swarming with disease-carrying mosquitoes, so the Brits had to sleep under mosquito nets. But they had to make sure the mozzies weren't in the net with them first!

7. For fun, a Brit in India might go on a tiger hunt. Great fun for the 'sahib' who got to shoot the tiger – but less fun for the Indian beaters who had to scare the tiger out of the jungle!

Heroes or Zeroes?

Here are a few famous colonials. Some say they were heroic, but to anyone with sense they were horrific!

SUICIDAL CLIVE

Robert Clive (or 'Clive of India') was a Brit hero who took control of most of India – and made a fortune while he was at it.

Clive went to Madras in India in 1743, where he worked for the East India company. He can't have liked the job much because he tried to kill himself … but failed.

Trunk luck

He got another chance to die in 1751, when he had to defend the city of Arcot against the French and Indians who wanted it for

IS THIS ELEPHANT WILD?

WILD? HE'S LIVID!

themselves. Indian armies sent elephants with spikes on their heads to batter down the city gates. Clive's defenders shot at the elephants. That didn't kill the poor jumbos – but it did make them very angry! The elephants charged the other way and trampled the Indians. Clive 'saved' Arcot – using the enemy's elephants!

Retired and fired

From then on the Brits used Clive as the chap to sort out any 'trouble' in India. He killed rebels in Calcutta, nabbed land from the French and bashed the boss of Bengal. Once his job was done he went back home to England … where he shot himself. Bang!

SAVAGE STANLEY

Henry Stanley was a 'hero' of the barmy British Empire. The truth is he was a real horror. But he's famous for a good deed – finding a man called Dr Livingstone who wasn't actually lost. The trouble was there were no phones or e-mails in those days, so the British people hadn't heard from Livingstone for a year. So Stanley was sent to 'find' him.

After walking hundreds of miles, through dozens of dangers, Stanley finally came across Livingstone and said those 'great' words…

DOCTOR LIVINGSTONE, I PRESUME?

Of course, Doc Dave SHOULD have said…

NO! I'M A MONKEY'S UNCLE YOU BRAIN-DEAD DINGBAT!

What did Stanley do next? Some deadly business that was more dastardly than daring…

Beastly business

Savage Stanley was hired by King Leopold of Belgium to help him rule the Congo area of Africa (the bit in the middle). Rubber tyres had been invented and the world would pay a fortune for the rubber that came from trees in the Congo. The world was also keen on ivory for billiard balls that grew on elephants in the Congo ... the ivory grew on the elephants, not the billiard balls. Horrible Henry set about his job with true Empire spirit.

Stanley had a talent for cruelty and greed. He...
• tricked tribes into losing their land
• forced children to carry huge loads
• had workers whipped to death
• had ears, noses or hands of rebels hacked off
• shot plenty of 'rebels' as well.

LETHAL KING LEO

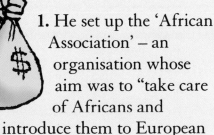

Leopold was Stanley's boss, the king of Belgium, and the nastiest of all the cruel colonials. He wanted the Congo as a colony of his own. And he got his mitts on it in some spectacularly sneaky ways...

1. He set up the 'African Association' – an organisation whose aim was to "take care of Africans and introduce them to European ways".

2. Then he tricked the other countries of Europe (and the USA) into giving total control of the Congo to the African Association...

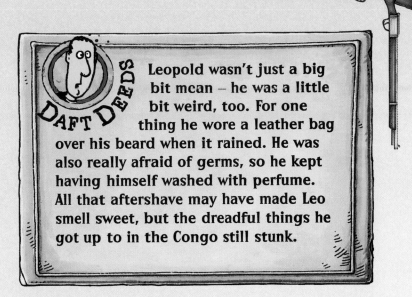

DAFT DEEDS Leopold wasn't just a big bit mean – he was a little bit weird, too. For one thing he wore a leather bag over his beard when it rained. He was also really afraid of germs, so he kept having himself washed with perfume. All that aftershave may have made Leo smell sweet, but the dreadful things he got up to in the Congo still stunk.

3. Of course, the Association was totally controlled by its chairman – bad King Leo!

He now had his own colony, which he called the 'Congo Free State'.

Free ... to suffer

But nobody in the Congo was free. And the only ways Leo 'took care' of the Africans was by making them work like slaves – or by shooting them.

Under Savage Stanley and Lethal Leo, over half the native people in the Congo died. But Leopold didn't care. He was rich! You might hope these two greedy sneaks got their comeuppance. Well...

DID THE DREADFUL DUO GET WHAT THEY DESERVED?

NOT QUITE... KING LEOPOLD DIED AS THE RICHEST MAN IN THE WORLD

BUT DIDN'T THE BRITS PUNISH HORRIBLE HENRY?

NOT EXACTLY. VICTORIA KNIGHTED HIM AND MADE HIM SIR HENRY STANLEY IN 1899 – AND THE BRITISH PEOPLE MADE HIM A MEMBER OF PARLIAMENT FROM 1895 TO 1900.

Cruel Congo

When King Leopold became boss of the Congo, the results were really horrific.